Victoria E. Henderson

I0385890

WHEN I NEED A WORD, GOD SPEAKS!

Studio Griffin
A Publishing Company
www.studiogriffin.net

When I Need A Word, God Speaks! Copyright © 2019 Victoria E. Henderson

All Rights Reserved. No part of this book may be used or reproduced in any manner whatsoever without written permission except in the case of brief quotations embodied in critical articles and reviews.

For information, contact:
Studio Griffin
A Publishing Company
Garner, North Carolina
studiogriffin@outlook.com
www.studiogriffin.net

Cover Design by Ruth E. Griffin
Photo by Victoria Henderson

This book is licensed for your personal enjoyment only and may not be reproduced, transmitted, or stored in whole or in part by any means including graphic, electronic or mechanical without expressed written consent of the author.

Scripture quotations marked KJV taken from The Holy Bible, King James Version. New York: American Bible Society: 1999.

Scripture quotations marked NIV taken from the Holy Bible, New International Version®. Copyright © 1973, 1978, 1984 International Bible Society. Used by permission of Zondervan. All rights reserved. The "NIV" and "New International Version" trademarks are registered in the United States Patent and Trademark Office by International Bible Society. Use of either trademark requires the permission of International Bible Society.

Scripture quotations marked Message taken from The Message: The Bible in Contemporary Language. Peterson, Eugene H. Colorado Springs: NavPress, 2002. Print.

Scripture quotations marked NKJV taken from The Holy Bible: New King James Version. Holman Bible Publishers, 2013.

Scripture quotations marked GNT taken from Holy Bible: The Good News Translation (2nd ed). 1992. New York: American Bible Society.

Lyrics, Turn Your Eyes Upon Jesus by Helen Howarth Lemmel, 1922. Public Domain.

First Edition

ISBN: 978-1-7361765-9-7

Library of Congress Control Number: 2019946414

1 2 3 4 5 6 7 8 9 10

Dedication

First and foremost, I thank God for choosing me to write His Words. I am changed forever because He loves me just that much!

This book is dedicated to all the women warriors who told me I could do anything I set my mind upon: Lisa Cooper, Leah Forney, Lori E. Henderson, Angela J. Williams, Valerie Evans, Valarie Brown, Sylvia Rogers, Keisa Stubbs, Dezrie Moore, Renita Sacknoff, Rahbyn Meyers, and my beautiful, wonderful mother, Lois E. Henderson. You spoke life into me and didn't even know it at times! You saw the best in me and never stopped coaching and loving me. You encouraged me to share my voice with the world. For this, I love you and I am forever grateful.

To Lorraine Hexstall and Avery Dawson: the harmony still runs deep in my soul. Thanks for giving me F.A.I.T.H. that endures.

To Beghetta Liles: you have been my cheerleader from day one. Your voice pushed me to accomplish what God would have me do. For always having my back and telling me the truth even when I didn't want to hear it, for praying over me, and loving me unconditionally, no questions asked! This one's for you!

To Courtney, Tanya, Parrish, Pamela, and Mervin: when we all get there... what a day that will be!! I miss you terribly.

I thank God daily for my babies, Vanaya, Varyssa, and Xireon. These writings exist because you do. You have motivated me to be everything God wants me to be! I pray I always make you proud!

May God add a blessing to the readers and doers of His Word!

Contents

Introduction	1
For I Know The Plans	3
I Need To Eat	6
What's So Good About It?	9
Because He Loves Me	11
Today I Cried	14
Inside The Fish	19
Outside the Fish	22
The Perfume of My Life	25
It's A Process	28
The Red Sea Experience	32
I Choose To Worship	35
Wouldn't Take Nothing For My Journey Now!	38
The Voice	42
Lord, Fix My Life!	45
A Scandal Only God Can Handle	49
I See ME	53
Love Is An Action Word	58
Orange Juice Praise	63
A Temporary Inconvenience!	68
Courage Not To Quit	72
Back To Basics	75
A Year In The Life	78
When God Speaks To You	83
Acknowledgements	91
About the Author	93

Introduction

Over the years, as I've faced life's challenges, I've found that writing has been a source of strength for me. I would send encouraging thoughts and messages to acquaintances and friends, and they would say, "You should start a blog!" So, in 2011, I created a blog called 'Still Waters'. Each of those blogs were God-inspired. At times, I would feel compelled to write even when I did not have a desire to write. There were some messages that came after I prayed and some as I was driving down the street. I would have to type my thoughts as soon as I got to a computer. I came to understand that God speaks to me in all circumstances, I just needed to listen! I always prayed someone would be touched by my words as I sent out a new blog; and each time, there was someone who said, "This was for me." Or "You blessed me more than you know." Those times brought me to tears because I always knew listening to God produced blessings beyond measure. Now I could see it. Their comments blessed me more than my words blessed them.

Compiling this book has been an emotional journey. As I read over what I wrote years earlier, I could feel the emotion of what I was saying and remembered my seasonal place as I wrote. I was struck by how relevant the writings were then as when I first penned them! I am in amazement of what God has and is doing!

This book is for all who wonder if God still speaks. He does indeed—in the conversation of a child, a sermon, a word someone says that sparks more deep thoughts, and through accidents that turn out to be more than just mere stumbling blocks. And He speaks just when we need it the most. You just have to be open to listening as never before. I pray this book encourages you to be still and listen as God speaks to you! Use the pages at the back of this book to capture your thoughts as you read.

For I Know The Plans
October 2011

For I know the thoughts that I think toward you, saith the LORD, thoughts of peace and not of evil, to give you an expected end.
Jeremiah 29:11 (KJV)

Two years ago, several of my friends encouraged me to take my writings and compile a book. So many told me the same thing at different times that I took them all in as confirmation that the Lord was talking to me. I needed to do this task. Topics came at me from left and right and I jotted them all down. I even dared to write a few missives and emailed them to my friends. However, I didn't move forward. I heard the call, but to tell you the truth, I doubted the Lord would want to use my words to encourage others. I was stuck in the "who-me-and-the-why-me" zone. Who was going to take me seriously when things in my life were not all perfect? Why would anyone truly believe that God talked to me by showing me parables in the simple things of life? That Christmas, a sister in my church gave me a devotional book for the coming year. The very first thought in the book centered around *Jeremiah 29:11. For I know the thoughts that I think toward you, saith the LORD, thoughts of peace and not of evil, to give you an expected end. (KJV).* Then, a dear friend, Angela

J. Williams, told me that I needed to share this very same scripture with my daughters to remind them that they were princesses in the kingdom of God, and He had plans for them. Yippee! Confirmation for real. I was on my way towards publishing!

NOT!

Two years later, another call has come. Now more than ever, I am compelled, drawn, and directed to write. As I watched the services for this year's Woman Thou Art Loosed conference through the Internet, I heard the Spirit tell me that I needed to share what was given to me with others. NOW! I cannot be sidetracked with the cares of life anymore. Nothing is more important than spending time with God and doing what He tells me to do. Will it be risky? Yes. Will everyone understand? Probably not. Will I face criticism? Maybe. But I have come to the point in my life that it does not matter anymore. Doing what God tells me to do is more important than what any man has to say about me.

Perhaps you have been there as well. Maybe you still are. You know God told you to go left but you went right. Like Jonah, going to Nineveh is not what you want to do. But also, like Jonah, I found that going in the wrong direction took me to places I never wanted to be in. My belly of the fish found me unhappy, unfulfilled, and out of the will of God. It has taken me two years to get back to the place where hearing from God is all I want to do. I am here now and excited to see where He will lead me. I encourage you today to spend time listening to the voice of God. What is it you are supposed to be doing? What is your calling and purpose? It is not too late!

Whatever your thing is, do it! I cannot promise it will be easy, but I know that obeying God will bring a sense of peace and purpose unmatched by anything else. God knows the plans for your life. Trust Him to bring to completion the good works He has begun in you. You will not be sorry! I know I am not.

I Need To Eat
November 2011

Jesus answered, "It is written: 'Man shall not live on bread alone, but on every word that comes from the mouth of God.
Matthew 4:4 (NIV)

I had a very real problem. I could not eat solid foods for a little over a week. My supervisor prepared a pre-Thanksgiving lunch feast of salmon. That night, my mouth was hurting and swollen but I ignored it. I prepared a second helping for lunch the next day as well. I did not let a little pain keep me from that plate on day two. Yes indeedy! That food was so good, and I ate every bit!

However, I paid the price. I developed an allergic reaction to the salmon. I'm not sure why but when I finally went to my dentist after almost six days of suffering, an allergic reaction was the diagnosis. During the time before the diagnosis, I doctored myself and probably made it worse. I was in pain and could not eat anything other than Jello, soup, and pudding. I was so hungry but could not tolerate anything being either too hot or too cold. The slightest touch sent me into throngs of agony! My gums were swollen, and my upper palate was like an open sore. It was truly horrible!

When the pain and hunger got the best of me, I decided to stop self-diagnosing and visit my dentist. He prescribed mouthwash and pain killers and by Thanksgiving I was able to eat again! Now you know I had a lot to be thankful for, yes Lord!

During that time period, I had some time to reflect on how much I needed God in my life. Just as I need food to eat, I require so much more of Him. I was not able to go to church like I usually did and that bothered me. My family went without me, while I sat home alone. Although I was able to watch the live streaming service on the internet, the experience wasn't the same. I thought about why I went to church and what it meant in my life.

The Bible tells us in *Hebrews 10:25 - Not forsaking the assembling of ourselves together, as the manner of some is; but exhorting one another: and so much the more, as ye see the day approaching. (KJV)*

I love to be in order and that sounds good—I do not forsake the assembling—I make it my business to find myself in the church house every chance I get. I have to admit, I don't do it just to adhere to this admonition to do so. I need to be in worship to hear the Word of God, just as I need to eat. I need to be among people who believe as I do so that when we come together, we are a force to be reckoned with in our counterattacks against the tricks of the enemy! Our corporate praise and worship will bring us into the presence of God and in His presence, miracles will happen. Healing, deliverance, burdens lifted—all of this happens as we worship. To hear the Word of God delivered in ways my mind never imagined gives me the courage and strength to face every challenge that comes my way.

Just as I need to eat food to gain my strength back, I need to feed off the presence of God in my corporate and personal worship to fulfill my calling and purpose. For me, playing church is over. I have determined to take my praise and worship to a new level. As I seek more of Him, I know God will show Himself strong in every area of my life. No turning back now!

I pray that you have found, or will find, a place to worship that helps you enter into His presence, that feeds you the Word like never before, and gives you the courage to walk into your purpose. I need to eat, don't you?

What's So Good About It?
November 2011

You heavens, praise him; praise him, earth;
Also ocean and all things that swim in it.
Psalms 69:34 (Message)

As I write this morning, tears are streaming down my face. Not tears of sadness but joy unspeakable! You see, someone asked me the title of this message and I started thinking about it until the joy consumed me. Let me back up.

I was walking into my building this morning after I dropped my girls off at daycare/school. I was dragging after our daily routine of morning fights to get out the door. Yet, in my Vickie way, I brightly said, "Good morning," to a young lady who worked there. She turned, looked me in the eye and said, "Victoria, what's so good about it? Tell me!"

I said, "Honey, there are a lot of things I can say that makes this day good: I drove myself here and I am walking into this building on my own, so don't get me started why it's a good day."

She walked away when I started my praise, but you know what, I kept on praising! All of a sudden, I felt the Lord's presence and I had to actually back out the door to bless His Name and get it together.

I told God, "I thank you for waking me up, even though I don't feel 100% today. I dressed myself! And I thank you for my kids, my husband and my family being healthy. Things are not as good as they could be for all of us right now, but You are still God and I know You are holding us in the palm of Your hands! I thank You for a job and people in my life who love me. I bless Your Name today for being God! For loving me in spite of myself! For saving me and giving me a greater understanding of Your mercy and grace! In every situation I will trust You and give You praise!"

Now can you see why the tears are still rolling? What's so good about it? I am a product of His grace which was amazing before I was even born! *Praise the Lord, oh my soul and all that is within me!*

You all have a blessed day and know that despite what the enemy brings against you, YOU ARE MORE THAN A CONQUEROR AND the devil IS ALREADY A DEFEATED FOE! We are not just winning; WE HAVE ALREADY WON!

Now, I have to go find me a corner to praise God a few more minutes!

Because He Loves Me
November 2011

But now, God's Message, the God who made you in the first place, Jacob, the One who got you started, Israel: "Don't be afraid, I've redeemed you. I've called your name. You're mine. When you're in over your head, I'll be there with you. When you're in rough waters, you will not go down. When you're between a rock and a hard place, it won't be a dead end— Because I am God, your personal God, The Holy of Israel, your Savior. I paid a huge price for you: all of Egypt, with rich Cush and Seba thrown in! That's how much you mean to me! That's how much I love you! I'd sell off the whole world to get you back, trade the creation just for you.
Isaiah 43:1-4 (Message)

I was feeling sort of low this morning. Thankful, yes, for another day, but pressed down in my spirit about how we would make the ends meet before the end of this month—and next month too, quite frankly (God is working with me on that anxiety thing, ya'll!). I was quietly listening to the radio, which was tuned to the local gospel radio station. After, "I WILL BLESS THE LORD" by Byron Cage and singing our hearts out, Vianna, my six-year-old, said, "Mommy, I love you!"

I answered back, "I love you too, sweetie!"

I had a sudden urge to ask her a question.

"Vianna, what does love mean, baby?"

She answered right away. "It means when you care about something so much that you want to take good care of it. Like, I care about my toys, and so I take good care of them."

Hold on, did my baby just teach me a lesson about God's love for me? I sat straight up and had to resist the urge to NOT pull my car over and break out into a run! I was so overcome that I missed the opportunity to tell her that her Father in heaven loves her so much, that He will always be there to protect and care for her. I admit, in that moment, I was totally selfish about this right here! In those words, came the naked truth of what God's love for me meant. He loves me so much that He not only sent His Son to snatch me from a hopeless future, but along my journey, He would take good care of me. Why? Simply because He loves me!

He loves ME—Victoria—with all my whining, crying, and anxiety-filled petitions. He has promised to take care of me and so through the words of my baby girl, I have to line my heart up with my head. Whatever comes, through every trial and blessing, because God loves me, He will take good care of me!

My day has picked up a lot since then. I got to work, and I began to praise His Name! My situation has not changed but I have been reassured that God is working for my good! I can't wait to get home and tell Vianna how much her God loves her!

Thank You Lord, for using the words of a child to show me that You are right here in the trenches with me and that Your love for me still covers all. I get so tired sometimes and need that extra push. Thank You for loving me enough to give me what I need exactly when I need it. Help me to trust even on the dark days! I love you, Lord, because You first loved me! In Jesus Name! Amen and amen.

Today I Cried

November 2011
For Doreen Wise – It Will Be All Right!

Thou tellest my wanderings: put thou my tears into thy bottle: are they not in thy book? When I cry unto thee, then shall mine enemies turn back: this I know; for God is for me.
Psalm 56:8-9 (KJV)

I am a self-proclaimed, self-help guru! If I even thought a book would help ease my inner struggles, it was mine! As a result, my library is packed with books that were popular in their time. Come on over if you want to borrow 'Your Best Life Now' by Joel Osteen (with the journal), Rick Warren's 'The Purpose Driven Life' (with the journal) or even 'The Secrets of the Vine' by Bruce Wilkerson (yep, with the journal). 'The Prayer of Jabez' book and journal have their place in my hallowed halls, and they would not be complete without any of the 'Woman Thou Art Loosed' series. Yes, I have the Bible, Devotional and prayer journal. I must admit when I bought them, I had very good intentions. I would read the titles and convince myself that if I would write my feelings down in those journals, my life would be miraculously changed because I took charge of my life and dared to help myself with these God-sent words! I hate to admit that some of these books look exactly like they did the day they were purchased.

Then I discovered Iyanla Vanzant and that was it! The titles alone made me run to get each one as they came out...'Faith in the Valley', 'The Value of the Valley', 'In the Meantime', 'Acts of Faith', 'One Day I Prayed', 'One Day My Soul Opened Up" (with the journal), and Yesterday I Cried'. Her words empowered and encouraged me to be more than what I was. That I was right where I needed to be at that point in my life but if I wanted more, I had to search inside myself. It was so good to me to hear words like this. I was struggling with who I was at that time and needed guidance and she was it. 'Yesterday I Cried' told her own story of humble beginnings and hurt as well as her path of discovery to what her purpose was in life. So, she cried yesterday but today was a new day for her. I cried because she made it through!

If I could find Ms. Vanzant today and have a fireside chat with her, I would tell her that her words helped me. Truly they did. But I was unprepared for what was ahead in my life after I read her books. And while she may have cried yesterday, and all was well, I cried a few yesterdays too. In fact, I have cried many days since I read her story and other books that were meant to send me on a path towards purpose and fulfillment. Foolishly, I thought once I read them, I wouldn't have to cry so much anymore.

But my tears help tell my story. You see, I cried the day I found out I was pregnant with my first child–I didn't think I could have children. I cried the day she was born and on the birth days of my next two babies. I cried when someone showed me kindness by giving me a small gift just for doing my job at work. I cried when my best friend preached her initial sermon, and I cried watching my children perform in their plays. I cry over sappy movies. I cry when my baby wraps her arms around me as far as they can go and says, 'Mommy, I love you!'

Just as much as I cried for joyous occasions, there were days when my tears were steeped in sorrow. I cried grasping my dad's hand as he led me down the aisle the day I got married. Two years later, I cried when I stood gazing in disbelief at his lifeless body in the hospital on the day he died. I cried the day I was told my mother was diagnosed with cancer. I cried many nights leaving her after her chemotherapy treatments and there was nothing I could do to stop her nausea and pain. I cry some days now when I see how she is not able to do all the things her mind wants to, but her body won't let her. I cried many nights (and still do at times) when depression creeped in with my frustration over life's challenges. These are hard days when I can't seem to stop the tears.

However, I can't seem to stop them either when I get to church and get to praising. As I lift my hands in worship, I realize that I am blessed to be able to sing, dance, and worship one more time. I marvel in these moments of gratitude for another chance to fellowship with God's people to the point where I cry. I can tell myself that this time, this service, I won't cry, but as my mind wanders over how I made it through the past week's trials or just simply at the goodness and holiness and awesomeness of God's love for me, I cry. I cried today, in fact, as I heard yet another message at church filled with blessings for my todays, hope for my tomorrows and goodbyes to the hurts of my yesterdays.

I have come to realize that my tears are indeed part of the process. They are the release that I need to let go of the emotions that are inside. They are a part of the promises of God that He keeps account of everything I go through, and at the end, the blessed end, MY GOD! They are mentioned as a ray of hope for us all. We have the hope that we can meet God and have Him personally wipe them from our faces. My God loves me so much that when I see Him face-to-face, He will take His Holy hands and wipe my tears away FOREVER!!

Hold on my friends! Know that your tears may fill buckets, but all is well! God sees you and understands exactly what you are going through. You are not ever alone. Cry when you need to—He will wipe them away and when He does that, you won't have to cry no more! That thought alone makes my eyes fill up even now!

And God shall wipe away all tears from their eyes; and there shall be no more death, neither sorrow, nor crying, neither shall there be any more pain: for the former things are passed away. Revelation 21:4 (KJV)

Inside The Fish

December 2011

(Another one from my archives! God is still working on us, ya'll!)

From inside the fish Jonah prayed to the LORD his God. He said: "In my distress I called to the LORD, and he answered me. From the depths of the grave, I called for help, and you listened to my cry.
Jonah 2 1-2 (NIV)

My brother asked a question that I turned around and asked the Lord: what is the Word for today? But I knew the answer already. You see, last week my children were watching a DVD in the van about different Bible stories and one of the stories was about Jonah. Yep, good ole Jonah, who lost sight of what God had called him to do and pursued his own course. As I listened to the kids' version and saw how my children reacted to the story and the songs, I heard the following question plainly as if someone was in the front seat with me: 'ARE YOU LIKE JONAH?'

I have been thinking about this now for about a week and writing down a few thoughts. The answer to that question is yes. I know I could be doing more for the gospel, but I sometimes let the cares of life hold me back. There is no time now for excuses; no time for, "I'll do better next week or next month". The time for change is NOW.

I re-read Chapter 2 of Jonah in the NIV version and loved it. Verse 8 stood out to me:

> *"Those who cling to worthless idols forfeit the grace that could be theirs.*

Wow! Here is that grace word again! As I cling to my idols of selfishness, perceived wrongs against me and ailments (the list could go on), I am losing out on the benefits of grace that could be mine if I surrender all, not some, to God.

Then comes verse 9:

> *But I, with a song of thanksgiving, will sacrifice to you. What I have vowed I will make good. Salvation comes from the LORD."*

My take on this: With a song in my heart and in my mouth, I will praise you although I'm still hurting (sacrifice of praise). "Inside My Fish" of worry, doubt and confusion, I will lay my burdens at the feet of the Master and leave them there. I will do what He says do and fulfill my vows to Him. When all this is done, I know my help is on the way and I will be saved!

Inside the fish, Jonah had a praise party all by himself! He praised in the muck of the nastiness in the belly of that fish and when he got out, he told anyone who listened that he had been in a pit of hell but when he called on the Lord his God, he was delivered onto dry land! So, am I like Jonah? Yes, yes, yes! I may feel alone at times, but I'm never forsaken! My troubles consume me and sometimes I feel beat up, battered and dirty, but I'm not without hope. I know God sees me and will deliver me into a place of dry land. I won't cry there or hurt anymore. So, while I'm inside this fish, I'm going to praise my way through!

Move over Jonah, Vic's dancing too!

Outside the Fish
December 2011
For Lorraine Hexstall – Friends for Life!

But it displeased Jonah exceedingly, and he became angry. So, he prayed to the Lord, and said, "Ah, Lord, was not this what I said when I was still in my country?
Jonah 4:1-2 (KJV)

My friend, Lorraine, had an awesome response to "Inside The Fish". Her words challenged me to look at the next phase of Jonah's life. I want to share a portion of what Lorraine shared with me.

> *Are we like Jonah? Here is the interesting thing…Even after the dance for forgive-ness, Jonah STILL had a problem being forgiving! He went on to Ninevah, delivered God's message, then got angry because he didn't see those dirty, rotten so & so's get theirs! If you have read any background about the people of Ninevah, you'll see that in OUR opinion, he might be justified for hating them. And in his lament to God you could almost hear our whining — "I KNEW it, that's why I ran away in the first place! I KNEW you were a compassionate, merciful God! But did they deserve mercy? We had been crying out to you for years to do something with this*

despicable race of monsters. Then you sent me over there (although it could have cost me my life) to deliver the message, "Repent or die!" I delivered it — okay, first I ran away — but I DID deliver it. And just because they had ONE joint prayer session, You forgive them! So, although Jonah could see HIS despicable, sin wrecked life, HIS need of repentance and expect God to give HIM grace and walk in faith believing that HIS one prayer could move God to forgive HIM...he could NOT extend that type of forgiveness or preach God's grace to those he considered "worse" than him. Mercy!

Good question, Lorraine...are we like Jonah? Do we forget sometimes that the same God who delivered us from our situations can deliver that boss who comes to work and takes his frustrations out on his employees? Can we not see that God can heal the heart of that church member who talks about us, touch the life of someone who cuts you off in traffic or bumps into you in the street? Can't God help us love when someone has done us so wrong it hurts, and you don't feel like praying? Trust me, I'm still working on that one!

I challenge us all today to remember that when we get "Outside The Fish" of our trials, the God that saved you and me can and will save the hopeless, the helpless, the untouchables, the less fortunate, those who are hurting, lonely, and in need of a Savior. He wants to use US to be a light to everyone whom we come in contact. And when we come out, we need to remember God's amazing grace toward us so that we can bring someone out too!

Now that's another real good reason to dance! And you won't be alone!

The Perfume of My Life
January 2012

Ointment and perfume rejoice the heart:
so doth the sweetness of a man's
friend by hearty counsel.
Proverbs 27:9 (KJV)

I absolutely love my 'smell goods'. This is what I call the various fragrances I wear. I admit I somewhat overdo it when it comes to my smells. If I can, I will get the whole line of a fragrance. I will bathe in the shower gel, use the lotion, then follow up with the perfume. I am on top of the world if it has a powder or talc in the line. You can't tell me nothing! I SMELL GOOD! And as many as I have, you would think I would not know if anything was missing, but I can tell immediately if something is missing or has been used. I know how I left the basket that holds my scents! You won't get one over on me!

A tad over the top? Maybe. I have come to realize that my passion stems from my childhood experiences once again. We only had one soap my mother would buy...that ugly yellow Dial soap. Ugh! In a family of six, it was inevitable that when it was my chance to bathe, someone would have gotten to the soap before me and there would be dirt and fingerprints all on the soap. I know someone can be a witness with me.

(smile) I vowed when I got older, I would not only NOT buy that yellow Dial at all, but I would have as many soaps as I wanted. As cleansing agents evolved, I fell in love with shower gels and rarely use soap these days. I also have a collection of perfumes and lotions that sit on my dresser and in a basket in my bathroom. I know for a fact, that I have had that bottle of Fred Hayman 273 since before my oldest child was born. She will be 14 in May, folks!

You see, my special stuff, my expensive treasures, are only used on special occasions. I use my cheaper stuff on a regular basis, but perfumes like the Fred Hayman are only to be used if I was going to a fancy party. I guess that's why I still have over half the bottle – not many balls, banquets, or fancy dinner parties for me. And it's ok.

As I looked at my collection the other day though, I wondered why I don't use my perfumes daily or more often. Why wait for special occasions? Each day is a special occasion! This new year is a special occasion. It is a new season for me, another chance to begin again. God has blessed my life in so many ways. I belong to Him. How do I know that? The Bible says in *Psalm 24:1, The earth is the LORD's, and the fulness thereof; the world, and they that dwell therein. (KJV)* I am in the earth and so I belong to the Lord. This makes me special, and each day I live is a special day. It is time I remember this fact on a daily basis and treat myself like I am His and He is mine. If I want to wear my perfumes, even the expensive ones, on any day, why not? Why should I not serve my kids their dinner on the special china (if I had some!)? If I continue to save that perfume for a fancy banquet, it may be another fourteen years before that bottle is near the end! What would be the purpose of that? To show I could save perfume?

Instead, it would show that I held materials things so close and so dear that I did not live my life enjoying every moment to the fullest. That, to me, would be a waste. So, I have determined that I intend to make this year the beginning of new things truly. I will wear my best perfumes daily as I strive to walk into the purpose God has for me. I will look my best when I walk out my door because I do not have to look bad to prove to the world that I am going through. I will smell my best, look my best, and be the best Victoria I can be. More importantly, I will pray that each day I can reflect the character of Jesus in all my interactions. I want to show everyone I come in contact that the love of Jesus in me smells better than any perfume I own.

It's A Process
March 2012

*And it came to pass in **process** of time...*
Exodus 2:23 (KJV)

*And it came to pass in **process** of time...*
Judges 11:4 (KJV)

*And it came to pass, that in **process** of time...*
2 Chronicles 21:19 (KJV)

Lately, it's just been one thing after another as I splash through this life of mine. As soon as I think I am over one hurdle, another one pops up just as unannounced and crazy as the last one! And it's not just me! I have had people tell me of sudden job losses, health issues, financial messes, relationship issues, pressure to do well in school, various issues with children, and another issue I thought was pretty much dead—that dreaded church hurt (where someone in a church you love dearly hurts you to the core and you question whether this place is indeed the house of God or NOT!).

No matter the issue, I have found that stress, frustration, worry, doubt, fear, and confusion all feel the same for everyone! I may not have your issue and you may not have mine, but I am right there with you when you tell me how bad you feel.

I want this to be over NOW, Lord! I want to feel better immediately! I need this pain to stop! This trial needs to go away! I need a real break before the next one comes! Can I just simply live pressure-free for more than five minutes? Even as I type this, can You send an answer and a miracle so awesome, I will be able to just rest?

In the midst of my head spinning and my heart twisting, I must focus on the Word of God and what it says I should do. All I could hear in my head was, *it's just a process, it's just a process*. So, I looked up *process* in the Bible and the scriptures above came up. There are a few more but the words are almost the same. "It came to pass...in the process of time." My, my, my! I think I am getting it!

As divine intervention would have it, I was listening to T.D. Jakes before going to work as I typed this. He was talking about the story of Moses as a baby, how his mother fashioned the ark and put him in it to save his life. He laid in that ark and sailed on down the river and was saved! What Bishop Jakes said just jumped out at me and I knew God was talking once again!

"It is not about the storms you face, but what you are riding in through them!"

Whew! Is that not powerful?

As we reflect on the process, we know that we will have storms. Sometimes it's not really about teaching us a lesson.

> *I used to say that there must be something God is trying to teach me – patience, humility, perseverance, etc. But sometimes it really is just life! -Dr. Theodore Pikes*

This life is not easy at times and that is just reality. But how I navigate through the process will make all the difference. In riding through my storms, I choose to travel in faith. Yes, that thing that assures me that even though I can't see the end from the beginning, I know my Savior has it all in His control!

Yes, yes, yes! No matter the bill, the trial, the issue, the hurt (even that dreaded church hurt), IT'S ALL JUST A PROCESS! And it has to be seen through to the end. The scriptures tell us that in the process of time, certain things came to pass. I believe that about my life as well. In my basket of faith, Jesus will see me through to dry land and safety! In the process of time, I will see better days, I will have all bills paid on time, my children will continue to grow and learn and love the Lord, my hurts will dissipate, my health will improve, and all will be well. In this process, in this transition, my faith allows me to see the impossible! I believe that things will be better – it's already done!

Cry if you have to! Yell, scream, get it out! I know it's hard and it hurts! But when you have done that, get back into the game and hold your head up high! You shall live and not die! Praise God for where He has brought you and what He is bringing you through! We are resting in His arms, which is the safest place to be!

Remember always that to get through you got to go through! And when you get through, remember to reach back and help somebody else...

The Red Sea Experience
April 2012

And Moses stretched out his hand over the sea; and the LORD caused the sea to go back by a strong east wind all that night, and made the sea dry land, and the waters were divided. And the children of Israel went into the midst of the sea upon the dry ground: and the waters were a wall unto them on their right hand, and on their left.
Exodus 15:21, 22 (KJV)

My sister and I were talking earlier today about life. Just plain life. We have different challenges, yet the feelings are the same…frustration, a little fear, uncertainty about the next moves to make, how in the world did I get here and how do I get out?

As I was encouraging her, I found I was talking to myself too.

"Hon, we are at our own Red Sea experience. We are right on the banks of the river…can't go forward and can't go back. Indeed, we are exactly like the children of Israel! They had been delivered out of Egypt in a mighty way. They had walked and walked with all their belongings until they got to that Red Sea."

Then a panic set in.... what in the world? Now, how are we going to get through this? I can't paddle over that, I can't do a decent backstroke or front stroke for that matter! I am too old to try to...better yet, and I am too tired! Why did God bring me this far only to have me die in this water? Doesn't He see me drowning? I think I was better off staying in Egypt with those nasty slave masters instead of getting my hopes up for a promised land! Now all I see are these high waters.

If you are at your Red Sea like me, all you can see is the high waters of your problems and issues. You have done all you can. You have walked and carried the burden as far as you can. You can't move forward, and even inch backward. What do we do when we feel overwhelmed like this? We see that God has delivered before. What about now? What do we do?

We simply stand still! And we do this because we know the end of the story! Praise God! The Israelites did not die in that place, and neither will we! BLESS THE NAME OF THE LORD!

> *And Moses said unto the people, Fear ye not, stand still, and see the salvation of the LORD, which he will shew to you today: for the Egyptians whom ye have seen today, ye shall*

see them again no more forever. The LORD shall fight for you, and ye shall hold your peace. Exodus 15:13, 14

So, I say to you, I say to my sister, and I say to myself, stand still and see the salvation of the Lord! He will fight for us! This problem, this test, this issue, you will see it again no more! Glory to God! I tell you, I am praising Him right now and crying as I type because I have the assurance now that everything is surely going to be all right!

I did not plan to write today but it's just here! I will bless Your Name at all times, God! For You are more than worthy to be praised! Glory! Hallelujah! I have laid this burden down today! This battle is not ours! It is the Lord's! So, I simply stand right now, releasing my faith to know that He will make a way out of no way for me. He will do it for you too! Just stand still and believe!

As God would have it, as I was on my way to get my children from school, the song, Let the Church Say Amen by Andre Crouch and Marvin Winans, came on the radio. In it, Marvin says, "even if you are at your Red Sea."! Now tell me this isn't divine intervention. Listen to the song and praise God with me! God has spoken today and all I will say is amen! So, let it be!

I Choose To Worship
May 2012

But when David saw that his servants whispered, David perceived that the child was dead. Therefore, David said unto his servants, "Is the child dead?" And they said, "He is dead." [20] Then David arose from the earth, and washed and anointed himself and changed his apparel, and came into the house of the Lord, and worshiped. Then he came to his own house; and when he required, they set bread before him and he ate. [21] Then said his servants unto him, "What thing is this that thou hast done? Thou did fast and weep for the child while it was alive, but when the child was dead, thou did rise and eat bread."
2 Samuel 12: 19-21 (KJV)

The story about David lamenting over the life of his child gives me so much encouragement. And this is what I need today to make it! I have nowhere else to run to but the Word of God! And when I run, He answers me and gives me what I need to run my race a little longer!

You may question why this story spells encouragement for me when David was fasting, praying, virtually standing in the gap, asking God to spare his son, his child, his little boo-boo, the child of his lust. David had sinned, and the child was now sick unto death. Even in his sinful state and knowing what he had done to provoke the Lord's anger, David chose to seek the Lord and intervene for the life of his child. In that process of repentance and sorrow, he knew that laying before the Lord to show humility and surrender was the way to get his petition heard. With his precious one hovering between life and death, and the despair of his sin against God causing him mind-blowing agony, he fasted and laid before the Lord. David knew God was the only One who could do anything to change that death sentence for the boy. He did not call for the priests to do sacrifices or even ask the people he led to do a country-wide prayer and fast. In the midst of his sorrow and heartbreak, David chose to seek the Lord for himself.

That fact encourages me to seek the Lord through every issue I face. As I navigate through the nonsense and push through the pain that is my life at times, I too must choose to seek the Lord! And not just that, I see how David handled himself AFTER the decision was done! When his baby died, he got up from fasting, washed himself, changed his clothes and WORSHIPPED! Even with a grieving heart, he still blessed the Lord and lifted a praise to His Creator!

David shows me I have to choose to remember that regardless of whether I am crying or laughing, the Lord IS worthy to be praised! You see, he knew that the only One he could count on through everything that life threw at him, and the consequences that came as a result of his own bad choices, was God. HE WOULD BE WITH HIM THROUGH IT ALL!

David made the choice to command his soul to worship God, and I am doing the same! I can choose to sit and complain about things. However, doing this will only make me feel worse and depressed. I choose to worship today because my faith allows me to know that the God who loved how David sought after His Heart is the same God who can and will deliver me from my circumstances! Glory to God!

Choose to worship today! Choose to dwell on the goodness of God and not the magnitude of the issues you face! He is much greater than any problem. He sees you and will deliver you from every situation – in the good and the bad, worship, worship, worship!

Wouldn't Take Nothing For My Journey Now!

August 2012

Brethren, I count not myself to have apprehended: but this one thing I do, forgetting those things which are behind, and reaching forth unto those things which are before.
Philippians 3:13 (KJV)

I was blessed on Saturday, August 18, to celebrate 48 years of life on this earth. I was awakened at 6:30 am by a beautiful text from my supervisor telling me Happy Birthday and to celebrate and proclaim another year of life on this earth. As I read his words and THOUGHT of the goodness of God and how He had spared my life for another year, a praise formed in my spirit that was expressed in tears and words of thanksgiving from my heart.

I was grateful and I am still today. You see, last year I was not in the same place mentally that I am today. Overcome with the pressures of life, I felt compelled to go into work last year on my birthday believing that I had no other choice. As I sat in a meeting typing the minutes, I promised myself that I would no longer work on another birthday that God blessed me. So, this year, even though my birthday was on a Saturday, I took off Friday and celebrated all weekend!

We have to take the time to celebrate us! Many times, we push ourselves to the brink of exhaustion by falsely believing that the ship would sink if we did not show up to paddle the oars. The reality is that if you or I were to become sick and not able to show up, the job we do would go on and not sink indeed! They would find someone else just as capable to paddle and tread water.

I chimed in on a debate recently on Facebook discussing whether it was considered selfish to take care of one's self even if it meant you had to put yourself before others. One person thought that God wanted us to always put others first before ourselves, that this was showing love. I respect everyone's right to an opinion, but I could not agree with that one.

I commented, "This post is talking about taking care of one's self, so we can take care of others. He is not talking about the selfishness that makes you turn your back totally on all humanity. What he is saying is that there are times when you have to say no to things that are draining you, so you can be the best you. Check the scriptures, even Jesus became weary and took time to REST! It benefits no one if you give until you are no good to anyone. Yep, you must think of yourself first at times, so you can maximize your fullest potential in the calling God has placed on your life!"

It has been told to me many times that I must take care of myself better but for the first time in my life I am really taking it to heart. In two years, I will be fifty years old. My health issues could be better if I ate healthier and lost some weight. I have been working on that and I am proud to report that I am down about ten pounds now. This has been a feat to accomplish but I feel so much better!

As I sat and contemplated my life on Saturday, I realized that I am so abundantly blessed. I don't have everything I think I want or need, but I have so much more than many others. Most of all, I am in my right mind (well, most days anyway...smile) and have peace about a lot of things. My children are well and growing, I have people in my life who care for me and pray for me when things get rough. I am not homeless, helpless, friendless, and loveless; and for this and more I am grateful beyond words.

No, I wouldn't take nothing for my journey right now! I have learned so much about myself and who I am in God. I could never go back to the time when I felt I had to push so much that I made myself sick. I praise God even now for all His blessings and for loving me into a place where I can love myself.

To God be the glory for the great things He has done and will continue to do!

The Voice
January 2013

*My sheep hear my voice, and I know them,
and they follow me.
John 10:27 (KJV)*

Parents around the world will agree with me on this. How many times have you been in a crowded place and your kids were not with you, yet when you heard, MOMMY or DADDY, your head immediately turned in the direction of the sound? You just knew you heard YOUR kid's voice above the noise! You had to laugh at yourself because you knew exactly where your child was at that moment, and they could NOT be calling you!

Another parent moment is when you are in a crowd, and you hear a small voice calling you and you KNOW it's your child. I mean, there is no doubt that your baby is calling you, so you turn to discover the matter. How is it that you could tell this voice belonged to YOUR child? Amazing isn't it?

We recognize the voice of our children because we know them, and they know us. Living together, loving each other, and spending time with them enables us to know them intimately. I have often said that I KNOW my children, I know what each of them are capable of doing and I know what certain behaviors belong to each one. If you tell me someone did such and such, I can tell you who did what without you telling me the name. This comes from experiencing the good and bad sides of each child and learning their likes and dislikes.

In 2013, I long for the same relationship with my Savior. It is time I do His Will before my own and do it well. If He says go left, I will go left. If He says stop and stand still, STAND STILL I WILL! We truly have no time left for playing games with this thing called life. We need to take our Christianity more serious than ever before.

Just last week, on the same day, two of my friends called me to pray for them. I was humbled that they thought of me when they needed someone to pray! Who me? The same lady who feels always in the middle of a mess? The same one who at times talks a good game but inside is scared and seemingly on the edge all the time? Who am I that I could pray for someone else when I need prayer myself?

In my moment of self-doubt, God showed me that if I am His follower, I should be the one called on to pray. Who else can His people go to, if not me, a proclaimed believer in the One who can fix all things? I was reminded once again that it is not about me. I have no goodness on my own to do anything. But as I yield my will to His, as I listen to His Voice, and he tells me what to do, I CAN DO ALL THINGS!

Are we doing everything in our power to live out His purpose for our lives? Are we learning daily to weed out the noise of the world and hear His Voice above all others? How can I know His Voice? I know that I need to spend more time with Him intimately, so I can always know it is truly His Voice that directs my every step. I encourage you to do the same! We can make this year our best ever—living fully and completely in victory and service as we win others to Christ with our testimonies!

I hear Him calling me and my answer is completely and fully YES!!

Lord, Fix My Life!
July 2013

Purge me with hyssop, and I shall be clean:
wash me, and I shall be whiter than snow.
Psalm 51:7 (KJV)

Anyone who really knows me knows I love me some Iyanla Vanzant! Come look on my bookshelf and you will see a library full of her writings. Titles like "In The Meantime", "Faith in The Valley", and "One Day My Soul Opened Up" are there. These books helped me through some rough spots in my life. She is an author who can inspire and uplift with her wisdom because it is real and based on her own personal struggles in this journey called life. She decided to dedicate her life to helping others by being transparent of her own pain and struggles. I admit I was and am still drawn to her because of that. If she can find her purpose by helping others through their pain this is someone I want to be like.

She now has a show on Oprah's network called "Iyanla, Fix My Life". I watch in amazement how people will invite her into their life's stage and ask her to assist them in making their story better. Iyanla will get in their face and force the truth to surface. I have learned from her that I must be truthful with myself first before I can be truthful with others. I must be willing to look inside myself and understand where my hurt began. Only then will I comprehend what it takes to overcome the hurt so that I can move into my calling and purpose with ferocity.

As much as I love Iyanla and as much as I know that sometimes you do need human intervention, I had to wonder if I am guilty of looking too much to others to help fix what only God can. I am an avid believer that sometimes you do need professional help. So often people suffer in silence with depression and anxiety when talking to a counselor, pastor, or even a close friend who will be unbiased can help you overcome that. We have placed a stigma on seeking help that I hope to lift one person at a time. If you need help, go get it! I am not ashamed to say that there were times I felt like I was sinking fast and talking to someone helped me more than I could have imagined.

What I am talking about now is not asking God to help when He is the first person I should go to. I admit I thought I had to have my hands on someone tangible here. Someone in my face looking at me so I can see that they really heard me. Where was my faith? I know my walk with God is an ongoing process and at times, I know I was not always walking in His will. This made me question if He was really there and if He really heard my cry? As I watched the people tell Iyanla their most intimate secrets, it occurred to me that I needed to be able to talk to God like that! He is the One who created me and knew me before I even knew myself. He is my Alpha and my Omega, the Author and Finisher of my faith! If I can't tell Him what is going on with me and ask Him for guidance first, then I do not need to say that I believe in Him, and that Jesus died for me.

A new chapter is beginning in my life. I know that I am older and wiser now. I am stronger and better. This is not due to any goodness of my own but all because of God's grace! As we were praising God in church last week, I was given a short vision of my life at age sixteen. In that moment, He whispered in my ear that He kept me from that time to now and would continue to do so as long as I worshipped and focused on Him. I would need to do what He wants me to do! I may need my friends and family to pray for me at times and need to seek a counselor's help.

I am studying now to become one and I am praying I can be a help to someone who has hurt like me. But I also know without a doubt that before I can ask anyone like Iyanla to come and help, I must first cry out, LORD, FIX ME! I know when He fixes and blesses, I will not be the same again! Under the light of His mercy, grace, and love I will indeed be all that He wants me to be.

Thank you, Lord, for loving me even when I was unable to love myself. Thank you for changing me into who I am today. I know I have a way to go but I know You will be there every step of the way. It is You and me all day, every day and I will praise You and honor You with everything I am. In Jesus Name I pray! AMEN!

A Scandal Only God Can Handle
February 2014

In conclusion, my friends, fill your minds with those things that are good and that deserve praise: things that are true, noble, right, pure, lovely, and honorable.
Philippians 4:8 (GNT)

Ok everyone – I have YET another confession to make. I am addicted to the ABC series Scandal. Yep, I surely am I, along with all true Gladiators, watched from the very first episode the story of Olivia Pope and how she marvelously handles the scandals that seem inevitable in Washington DC. I made it my business to be sure I had done all my evening chores and routines so that I could be in front of the TV at 10:00 on Thursday nights. Well, sometimes I didn't even care about that, and things went undone, if I am honest about it. I waited with bated breath each week to see what would happen to her and how she and her team would get some poor sap out of the messes they found themselves. Even my fifteen-year-old daughter began to get attached. We watched together and had a good time bonding as we discussed the plots and "scandalous" behaviors.

My conscience would bother me a little, but I could not let it go. A Facebook friend, who watched as well and would participate in chats back and forth on Scandal nights, posted once that we as Christians really needed to stop watching Scandal. She did for a while, and I thought she was so brave to say how she felt and admonished us to be cautious in this arena. I did stop participating in the Facebook chats, but I did not stop watching. I was really struggling as I watched the last few episodes of Season 2. I loved the thought of a strong woman who can handle herself in a male dominated world. I loved Olivia's clothes and her snappy lines and her being in the thick of the political world, knowing who's who and the dirt on them all. I loved her ability to find out any piece of information she needed. But (you knew it was coming right?), I had to stop and think more about the things I do not like and how they are not lined up with the things of God and how He wants us to live. I admit also that the Holy Spirit has pricked my heart even more not to watch when my pastor was appalled at how he would see his members make comments on this program like nothing was wrong. He was so upset, he was ready to leave Facebook. His sermon the last Sunday of the final episode about this subject was confirmation for me that it is time to bow out!

As much as I loved Olivia Pope, the truth is in two seasons she has slept with three people, and one was married and not leaving his wife for her. What messages was this sending to my fifteen-year-old? Would she think it was ok since it was a show so loved by her mom and so many others? Would she further equate my past with being as glamorous as the life of Olivia Pope?

With this in mind, I will not be tuning in tonight for the opening of Season 3. I have simply had enough. I must take into account that in this season of my life, as I am struggling with my own aloneness, I cannot watch Olivia Pope or anyone else bed hop. I am trying to live a better life in front of my girls as I seek to fulfill God's purpose in my own. Dwelling on who is doing what to whom will not help me achieve the goals I have set for myself. Watching this show will not help me keep my mind off of wanting to be kissed and held as I see Olivia being embraced.

No, I am not trying to be holier than thou, spoil anyone's entertainment, or pull down the rating on a show that is number one right now. What I am doing is admitting that I have had some scandals of my own. I have not always been a good girl. I have been downright messy. But in the midst of all that, God reached down and loved me anyway! He took me from a very dark place and placed me in the light of His love and grace. I cannot, I simply will not go back to a place that says anything goes and it's just a show. God handled my scandal, and I am telling Him and showing Him that I mean to stay in this better place. My scandalous days are in the past and in order for them to stay there, I must be careful of what I watch. As I grow to be who He called me to be, I must be careful of what my kids see me watch and what they see me do.

I am also continuing my education. If I can dedicate so much time to a TV show, I can dedicate time to reading my textbooks, talking to and sharing with my kids and better yet, spending time in prayer and worshipping the God who saw my scandal and handled me the only way I could have been saved – He loved the hell right out of me! Go on now Olivia, go on! *I am a Glad Gladiator for God!*

I See ME
March 2014

But we all, with unveiled face, beholding as in a mirror the glory of the Lord, are being transformed into the same image from glory to glory, just as by the Spirit of the Lord.
2 Corinthians 3 (NKJV)

I attempted to write this blog without crying but the tears are already here. Being honest with yourself is not easy or comfortable but it is necessary if you are to learn a lesson from your pain, grow from the experience, and then have the strength to move beyond that moment to greater heights. I had such a moment on February 22, 2014. I was spotlighted as the character I portray in the production my drama ministry presents every 4th Sunday, and this was my month to have my character's personality showcased to the audience in our ongoing monthly saga. I learned my lines and did what I had to do. Everyone said it was done well by all participants and my cast members and I looked forward to the next few months keeping this ministry alive and well at our church. My issue was simply that I am overweight and not healthy. If I do not change how I live and what I eat, I will not see my children grow up and that is a reality. I watched my performance and was and still am horrified by the image that anyone who clicks on the link to the archives of our services saw. There I am in my costume, and it is a me I don't know. How did this happen? When did this Victoria appear? Is that really how I look? Is that really how people see me, so wide and stretched out? Can people see how out of breath I get when walking? Do they see my swollen ankles and the pain of my fibromyalgia that I try to hide with my nice clothes and makeup?

That picture of me and some recent health issues sent me to my doctor. I have inquired about gastric bypass surgery and although we agree that it can be an option, a better option right now is for me to begin a regimen that will include an appetite suppressant, seeing a nutritionist, and walking for twenty minutes three times a week to start. I will see him again in six weeks to see where I am and if I have succeeded in tipping the scale in the downward direction. I have to be open with myself and you that I am beginning this journey at 253 pounds on this five-foot three-inch frame. I don't mind sharing because I have determined that it will not always be this way.

The expression, "I SEE YOU" is used to acknowledge the physical presence or accomplishment of someone when they would not otherwise be noticed. It also hails from the movie

'Avatar', where the Na'vi people say it expresses their love to each other, in a natural and in a spiritual sense on how they were all connected. To be seen by the other was to know that they were together in the journey of life, and all was well. It was a way of saying that one exists and is here because the other has confirmed their existence by seeing their heart, soul, and the love that is between them.

I get that. It is beautiful to be acknowledged by others. It is wonderful to get applauded and affirmed by the world. It is important to connect with something outside of yourself and to know that you matter to others. Yet, I am convinced that in this season of my life, I need to see ME! I have no other choice but to get real about why I eat out of frustration and depression. I must deal with the pain I let no one see as I think about the choices I made that have left me with three children to raise as a single mother. I have to look inside my hurts and deal with them in ways that are no longer detrimental to my health and happiness.

No, this is not a time for feeling sorry for myself or regretting the past. This is the time for honest appraisals of what I can do to be better – a better woman, a better mother, a better servant being about God's business. I have to see the me that was abused, mistreated, abandoned, and feels unloved. I have to see beyond that person to see how God sees me. I have to speak to that part of me and tell her she is okay; she is safe in the arms of the One who created her to be and do so much more. There was a time in my life that feeling bad about myself was second nature to me. I felt so abused and unloved that I believed what was happening to me was actually my fault since I had made the choice to be in certain situations. These choices meant that I had to stay stuck. It was my punishment.

I found deliverance when I listened to a song called Mercy Saw Me. Some of the lyrics spoke to me so vividly that I began to weep until I felt God's presence love me back.

As I began to understand that I must see myself through the eyes of the greatest love of all, I see me healed, happy, and whole! Just like back then, apply this thought to my life today. God sees where I am, and the wonder of it all, He loves me anyway. I will rely on His strength to show me what I need to work on and the ability to keep it going despite feeling weak.

Realizing that I cannot do His business in this raggedy temple and making the much-needed adjustments to be healthier, mentally, and physically, I have begun to eat better and have been drinking only water. I am taking my medicines as prescribed and on time. I am on day four or five, but who's counting? Each day will be an exciting journey for me as I tread back to the me I used to be. I see me running in the park with my kids. I see me smiling as I have to get new clothes since the 24s are way too big. I see me throwing some of these pills away because I will not need them anymore. I see me singing, holding notes, raising my hands high in praise as I thank God for the new chance to live the rest of my life as healthy as possible. I see me leaving depression, guilt, and negative thoughts way behind me. I see me and I am beautiful.

Please do what you have to do to take better care of you! We only get this one life, so make it the best it can be for you and those you love. I SEE YOU!

Love Is An Action Word
April 2014

This is how we've come to understand and experience love: Christ sacrificed his life for us. This is why we ought to live sacrificially for our fellow believers, and not just be out for ourselves. If you see some brother or sister in need and have the means to do something about it but turn a cold shoulder and do nothing, what happens to God's love? It disappears. And you made it disappear.
I John 3:16-17 (Message)

Lately, I have been hit with some serious challenges as a mother of three growing and changing girls. What in the world happened to my darling babies who I dressed up, held in my arms, and cried when I had to leave them anywhere? When did they turn into people who could hurt me with shrugs of the shoulder, dirty looks, and below standard work at school and at home not even close to the potential that lies within? When did I join the ranks of parents who had reason to complain about kids who have suddenly turned into monsters they didn't recognize? When did it turn, Lord? You set me up when they were born! The past week, I seriously struggled with this new pain and cried more days than one over what to do, what is my part in creating this mess, how could they do this to me when I do so much, and being real, Lord, help me not to be resentful and regretful over how this life of mine has turned out!

I can tell you for myself that when you seek the Lord, He will answer. I can also testify that it may not always be the answer you think it will be, but the Lord will comfort you as only He can! In the midst of my crying, whining, and complaining, He gently reminded me of the love He has shown to me and how I must now extend that same love to my children and anyone else who has hurt me.

More and more, I am convinced that LOVE is more than a four-letter word. Recent events in my life and the lives of those close to me have shown me how people can say they love you and do quite the opposite. I have also seen acts of pure unselfishness being done and not a word was spoken. What motivates some to show love and others to just say it? Sometimes the way some people act towards you makes you declare that they could not possibly love you at all! But what I discovered to be fact is that love is present and real whether you feel it or not. In my most unlovable state, God extended His love towards me and gave me a chance to live a new life in Him. He did not base His love on whether I loved Him back or even cared that He loved me! He simply loved and protected me despite me. My Savior had me on His mind when He took on this world and died for me, saving me from a death without the hope of a future with Him!

This I know but God had to remind me again of how despite the great mess I have been, He loved me through the process as I now must do with my children. I did not fully understand or appreciate His great grace until much later in my life and neither will they understand the lessons I am trying to teach them until they experience life outside of the cocoon I have built around them, which is coming sooner than they think! If I say I love them, I must correct what I see wrong quickly and firmly but with the thought in mind that discipline is part of the process. They must learn life will not always be peaches and cream. If I love them, I will not allow them to believe that their actions do not affect others. They have to see that they do not live on an island to themselves but are connected in such a way that everything they do affects everyone around them. That regardless of how young they are, their actions will affect them for the rest of their lives.

This love thing is deep, my friends! We cannot say we love someone and then, seeing them in pain or suffering in any way, or going down a wrong path, do nothing! We cannot allow how we feel to prevent us from extending the same grace shown to us. Loving someone despite how dirty their sins are or what they do to us is not an easy task. This I know to be true for myself. Loving someone while you know they do not have your best interest at heart is a hard thing! How do you love when your first instinct is to run? How do you love when the hurt comes from those who are the closest to your heart? How do you love family members who say mean things, church members who are supposed to uplift you but fall down on the job, spouses who do not understand you, children who are still immature and hurt you to the core?

All I can suggest to you is Jesus! We used to sing a hymn by Helen Lemmel whose 1922 lyrics state, *Turn your eyes upon Jesus, look full in his wonderful face, and the things of earth will grow strangely dim, in the light of his glory and grace!*

- Focus on Jesus – study His examples of love in the face of people He knew would betray and kill Him!

- Focus on Jesus – see Him heal people who He never saw again that we knew of!

- Focus on Jesus – watch Him heal the ear of one of the very guards sent to arrest Him!

- Focus on Jesus – ponder over Him washing the feet of Judas, and seeing Peter deny Him. He still had words to comfort Peter's heart that restored him to his rightful place, while He Himself was incarcerated!

- Focus on Jesus – hear Him love a thief into eternal life!

My God, tears are rolling as I write this and begin to focus on Jesus! I pray right now for you and for me. I pray God will give us the strength to endure and love someone out of their sins and into the place where God can use them for His glory! I pray I can do this, not just for my kids but everyone I come in contact!

In this Easter season, may the power of the Resurrection be more than a story but a time of renewal for us to truly show love in action in all we do! Blessed be the Name of Our Lord and Savior Jesus Christ!

Orange Juice Praise
June 2014

That the trial of your faith, being much more precious than of gold that perisheth, though it be tried with fire, might be found unto praise and honour and glory at the appearing of Jesus Christ.
1 Peter 1:7 (KJV)

It's been a while, I know! I appreciate all of you who hang in there with me when I am silent. I do not mean to be but there are times when the encourager needs encouragement. Then God gives me a message so clear, I can't wait to get to typing. Today is such a day! I want to be silent but cannot dare go against what God has placed in my heart to share. Sorry it's been so long but you will see why!

The past few months have been more than rough. In fact, this whole school year has been a tough one for my middle child as she has fought to find her place in the world and adjust to the pressures of seventh grade. I have been to her school numerous times for behavioral issues, including a few fights that stemmed from being bullied. This has left her feeling less than. If you saw her pictures or spent time around her, you would think she is a happy, friendly girl—and she is, but she had become really good at masking her true feelings.

All of this came to a head about two weeks ago, when I discovered she had been engaging in self-harm behaviors as a way of coping with her inner pain. For any parent, to see signs of self-harm on your child has the effect of a stabbing in your heart. One bout of crying won't ease it. In fact, several bouts won't take it away either. I find myself constantly crying at the drop of the hat. I did not want to share this, nor did I want to be transparent. I did not want to tell the world about a private pain. I did not want to admit that this was happening to us; and have cried bitter tears and prayed that God would spare my baby, my innocent little girl, from feeling so bad about herself. How could she feel at twelve that there is no hope? What have I done or not done to show and tell her about how real Jesus is? This is not happening to us....it just can't be true, and I don't like it!

Despite my dislike, I have pressed forward in seeking help for us all. I am seeking more intensive counseling for her and am loving her back to herself with patience and understanding. As a family, we will be in counseling to support her and gain understanding of how to help her. God alone can and will heal and deliver, but the truth is that I, too, have hid behind my own pain for too long masking it with food, denial, jokes, makeup and clothes while the hurt festers in a dark place I do not care to see. Could she and her sisters somehow feel what I try daily to hide? Were they, like I was fighting the process?

Here comes the revelation!!

Today, my cup of orange juice spilled on my desk and in that moment, God spoke to my heart. I had been praising at my desk and made a sudden move that knocked over the cup of about eight to ten ounces that I never had a chance to taste. It went into my drawer, started dripping into the next one, on the floor and all over my desk. As I sat there stunned, it occurred to me that I could either fuss and cuss or continue to praise as I cleaned up the mess. Because no matter what I did, I would have to clean it. No one else was going to do it. So, I decided to keep on singing and started to clean it up. Then it hit me--there are some messes in my life that I have to clean up. Me – Victoria. No one else but me could do the work to be healed completely. But I had to choose to do it and choose to keep on singing and praising through the process. Not begrudgingly or fighting the process but knowingly with a calm assurance that even though I don't like the process one bit, it is necessary for me to be clean and whole.

But there's more. This is the next revelation!

The orange juice had slipped through the cracks and into the next drawer. If I did not clean it up, it would go from the first to the second and on to the third one too. This is the same way we pass down disease from generation to generation – by not stopping and cleaning it up once it shows up. I have to be healed inside and out so that I do not pass on to my daughters that it is ok to hurt in silence.

That's not all. Here is the final revelation!

It took some time to clean the orange juice out of my desk. It soaked everything, and I filled a whole garbage can of messy items and soaked paper towels. What happened over a course of a few minutes took almost an hour and a half to clean up. I had to literally take some items out one-by-one, wipe them off to be used again or thrown away.

Lord, you are working on me today! Some things happened to me recently, but there are other incidents that occurred years ago that I have to deal with. Some of it has to be thrown away and some are lessons I need to use to pass on to my babies. I can be silent no more.

So today, I choose to do the work. I choose to praise my way through the process trusting God for an end that is expected to be glorious! My children will be healed and whole and so will I. That orange juice spilled for a reason which I did not understand at first. Once I chose to begin to pray and worship, God's light came shining through! Yes, I will cry. Yes, there will be some things discussed in counseling that will hurt. My babies will cry and that will hurt me too. But I am just as sure when it is all said and done, we will come out stronger and healthier than when we started, and this is reason enough for me to praise God that YET praise that started from the orange juice spill!

A Temporary Inconvenience!
October 2014

That as ye are partakers of the sufferings, so shall ye be also of the consolation.
2 Corinthians 1:17 (KJV)

I'm feeling joy today, my friends! It is the type of joy that cannot be explained because it is the joy of the Lord! I am still riding on the high I felt in church last week. We never got to the sermon of the day because of praise, worship, praying for healing, and an altar call for those who just wanted to get it right with the Lord. It was an experience I shall never forget, and I am sure other worshippers feel the same.

It has been like this lately at our church: God is in the midst of His people and that is giving me this joy that is truly unspeakable. I have heard from God in each service as never before and I know in this season He is doing a new thing in me. For example, I somehow "lost" my charger for my phone in church and surprisingly I was not as upset as I normally would be. To lose something that I have no funds at all to replace would usually put me in a tizzy. I would pout, cry, and tell the world I had been robbed! Initially, I was upset and put out, but this great God we serve whispered something precious to me. He said, Baby, this is just a temporary inconvenience!

WOW! Ok, Lord, I hear YOU! How can I be upset over a charger when I witnessed the power of the Holy Ghost move people to surrender their lives to Jesus? So, what did it matter that my phone would die? I would be ok! So, what indeed! What is that in comparison to telling others there is a God who loves them so much He gave His Son for them and gave them another way to live that did not include sin, depression, guilt, and bitterness!

This led me to think about the past few months of my life. I have shared that my daughters and I had to go into counseling. I resisted it with every fiber of my being. I did not want to admit that I needed help right along with them; and I certainly did NOT want to expose our secrets to outsiders. I did not want to have them come into my house and open up wounds that had been festering for years. I did not want to do the work that it would take to clear our hearts and minds of self-esteem issues, anxiety, and depression. I did not want to admit that my precious babies even had issues to discuss. Not mine, no way!

However, no matter what I did not want, what remained to be true was just that—the truth! And truth had to be told and dealt with. We have done just that, are continuing to do so even now. We have cried, we have prayed, we have talked about it, opened our minds to thinking about things in ways that we didn't before. We were temporarily inconvenienced! We were nudged out of our comfort zone so that we could see the real truth about our issues and deal with every last one.

What I did not want to do had become my only way out! Being inconvenienced for a little while has meant healing and growth for me and my babies! I have seen them go from being angry and distant to laughing and sharing more with each other. They have stopped being isolated at home and actually seeking each other out for talks and playing together. One day driving down the street, I heard them laughing to tears together about something silly and it was music to my ears! I found myself laughing too. All I could do was simply tell my God, THANK YOU!

I encourage you today to embrace your inconveniences! Our God has a better plan for you if you stick it out. Trust that He has it all worked out and when you come through it, you will understand why you had to be temporarily put out of your comfort zone! We may suffer a little now, but the consolation is going to be, oh so good!

PS: When I get another charger, I will ensure that it stays in my bag!

To God be the glory!

Courage Not To Quit
November 2015

Be strong and of a good courage; be not afraid, neither be thou dismayed: for the Lord thy God is with thee whithersoever thou goest.
Joshua 1:9 (KJV)

Hello my friends. It's been a while, I know! So sorry! I have not forgotten you at all. I pray this post finds you in good health and in a position to finish this year strong in faith and pressing towards the mark. I have sat down to write so many times and I could not do it. I wanted to but the words could not form without tears and each time I stopped. I had given up my will to write. You see, this year has been a sad one for me. I lost a very close friend in January. Someone shot him in the head – point blank. In an instant my friend of twenty-seven years was gone. This blindsided my heart in ways I am still trying to cope with. In addition, my mother-in-law passed away in February, while my own mother has been in and out of the hospital about four times this year. A cousin passed, an uncle too. Then, another friend of mine died suddenly at the age of 48. Then just about a month ago, my best friend's brother passed away at the age of 45. There has been so much loss this year. Just one thing after another. The stress and heartache have been a lot to bear.

Ok, the tears are here again but I am determined to finish what God has told me to do.

He impressed upon my heart that, as always, I must share my story to help someone else. I have to tell you how He graced me with courage not to quit. The sadness has threatened to overwhelm me to the point that I didn't care much about anything anymore. I got up and went to work, took care of my household but would cry myself to sleep at night and before they woke up in the morning. I could not understand why my friend was taken in such a violent, horrible, and senseless way. I did not question God in anger saying, how could You let this happen, but I did ask, why Lord, why did it have to happen this way? I just simply don't understand! I just want to talk to my friend!

I realized there are some things in this life that will never be explained. I can question all I want but there is no sense to things that are senseless, and those answers are impossible to get. I asked God to help me bear it, to make the day come when I didn't feel like there was a weight on my chest.

Yet somehow, some way, I am able to face each day knowing that God is surely with me. The words spoken to Joshua so long ago are my mantra – AS I WAS WITH MOSES, I AM WITH YOU! (Joshua 1). That is exactly how I am making it each day, telling myself that no matter what, God is with me! Through it all, through the days when I am sad, the days when I do find something to smile about that truly makes me smile and not feel fake. Through the days when I want to slap my children for doing something silly, days when I don't feel well and am in pain. Through every situation, my faith sees and knows my God is ever present and holds me in the palm of His Hand!

I have courage not to quit today because that something within me gives me strength, day to day, to hold on and press forward. His Name is Jesus – Who is indeed the Author and Finisher of my faith! He is my Solid Rock, my Way out of no way, my Comforter, Redeemer, and Friend. O magnify His Name with me today! I thank Him for wiping away each tear and giving me strength to carry on His purpose in my life! Don't quit either my friends! We have come too far to turn around now! Remember – WE WIN!

Back to Basics
October 2017

But without faith it is impossible to please Him, for he who comes to God must believe that He is, and that He is a rewarder of those who diligently seek Him.
Hebrews 11:6 (NKJV)

I had a conversation with my sister last night about what to do when you are in situations that make you feel a bit on the helpless side. What do you do when you know you need to let go and can't seem to do that? You say you trust God, but you find yourself still worrying and still trying to solve it with your limited view and thinking.

As we were about to say good night, I told her, sis, the beginning, and end of it, is to pray. To take it to God and ask Him to fix it, to bear it, to direct, guide and comfort as only He can.

This resonated in my heart for my own situations, and I woke up this morning determined to do just that: Practice what I preach – take it to God! This led me to question myself, Lord, do I truly believe? Wow! Immediately Hebrews 11:6 came into my head: if I even come to God, I must first, FIRST, have to be sure in my heart that He even exists. I have to know with no doubt that the God I serve, the One I pray to, is real. And this, my friends, is how I will begin to let go, how I will begin again in Him. Back to basics, if you will! How can I even pray if I doubt that God exists? And if I doubt that, what assurance do I have that He is in control? It's all in the faith factor!

I have to believe that all is working for my good. I have to walk in faith and not doubt that He will reward me as I diligently seek Him. So, I must diligently do the work that is my part of the deal. I must activate my faith and seek Him as never before. I, Victoria, must praise Him and worship Him as if my life depends on it, because it does! In this season, there is no time for doubting or acting faint in heart. This really is the beginning and end of it, placing every situation that bothers me in the capable Hands of my Lord and Savior. I tell Him how I feel. I worship Him. I give Him my whole self in a life of service. I tell everyone, by word and action wherever I go, that there is a God in me who I trust with my life. In doing this, I let go of me. I let go of whatever control *I think* I have and allow God to do His part. I concentrate on bringing more of God into my life. I listen to His Word and mediate on that Word and allow praise music to lift me above the troubles of this world (which really is not my home). Simply put, it is back to basics – trusting, hoping, believing and activating faith until it appears.

We must do it! When we believe that God is, that God is – think of it – GOD IS! And because God is, everything we face is working for our good! GOD IS! I am gonna press on a little longer and bask in His goodness and mercy towards me, because God is all I need!

A Year In The Life
December 2018

But thou art the same, and
thy years shall have no end.
Psalm 102:27 (KJV)

Well....it seems I have let the entire year of 2018 go by without writing. I did not reach out to you, my friends, and I am sorry for that. I have missed you! I honestly didn't mean to go this long without writing. The truth is, I was embarrassed and ashamed of what I was going through.

I have been very unhappy most of the year and when I tried to write, I just couldn't do it. I would think – who really wants to hear that I am sad, depressed, unhealthy, and sick of this life I was living? How can I encourage God's people when I need this myself? I was just at a crossroad, and I let my self-pity stop me from doing what God has compelled me to do. I took myself out of His will for me and let my feelings get in the way of doing what I love to do and what I am called to do.

I have to be fully transparent because that is the only way I know how to be. I also have held up my book release due to fear. I actually felt that I could not possibly release a book of hope and encouragement when I felt so hopeless and defeated most days. Who would want to read my stories and how could I even hold my head up when all I wanted to do was run and hide?

I was in a bad place, and I cried and worshipped and still praised God through it all. But, I still didn't move. I went to counseling, prayed, and cried and still didn't move. In October, I attended my high school reunion and even though I enjoyed seeing my folks from back in the day, I was miserable – in body and spirit. I was not in good health and smiled the whole time feeling so sad. I had a heart to heart while there with one of my best friends in this world, Dezi Moore. I told her how I was feeling, and she told me, Vic, it's time for you to take care of you. Do what you have to do to be sure you are ok and living the life you want to live. I watched as she laughed and enjoyed the moments of simply being when she had just come through one of the most challenging and painful health scares this year. It was simply God's grace and mercy that she was even there with us, and we had a blessed time indeed.

Seeing my old friends and being able to laugh with and share days of love with them changed me in a profound way. I realized that I had to take better care of myself and let go of things I was upset about but could not change. I came home with such a renewed mindset to change some things and I did just that. I began to eat healthier, and I lost eight pounds. I, along with Dezi and some other friends, joined a weight loss group where we challenge and support each other and have lost another 8 pounds. I have begun to exercise, and it's been hard but it's so worth it to see and feel the changes in my body and mind.

I sent my manuscript to one more person to read through for me, but I still procrastinated. On December 14th, I attended a banquet at my church and sat next to precious Elder Andrea Hines who let me ask questions about her writing history. I shared my fears with her, and she told me, "Victoria, remember, everybody is going through something. Your writings will help someone who needs to see what it looks like to go through and make it!" She doesn't know how much that impacted me and the tears I shed on the way home.

Well, God and I had a talk and in His loving way, He has forgiven my doubts and procrastination. The book is with my publisher and friend, Ruth, for the final lookovers and I have done my part as we walk in the final hours of 2018.

This year has not been easy for me, my friends, not even a little bit. But this I know – my God was with me on January 1, and He is with me even now. He knows the end from the beginning, and He knew I would find my way back to His loving arms. Not because I have been good, but because He is good, and His mercy endures forever. Once again, He has taken my mess and turned it into a message. This message is full of love and hope for my bright future!

And it's for you too! God's grace, which is still amazing, rings true in the scripture above! David proclaimed that He is the same, and His years have no end! Yep, here comes the tears! I may have needed this year to get it together, but He knew that already and was with me in January, July, and December. Waiting for me to realize once again that I can do all things through Him. I believe! Help the parts of me, Lord, that will doubt Your power to heal and restore in the days to come!

I proclaim 2019 will be a victorious year for us all! There can be no doubt that "that he who began a good work in you will carry it on to completion" (Philippians 1:6, NIV). I may not know what will happen or have control over much of it. But I do know more than ever that God is gonna be with me every step of the way. Cry, scream, yell, but don't stop moving forward!

I pray that this coming year will have us all experience more of God in miraculous ways! Happy New Year, my friends! Welcome to a new road on the journey!

Still Living Victoriously!

When God Speaks To You

The following pages are just for you! Perhaps you hear God speaking to you too and need to jot it down now! You can also use these pages to write down your thoughts on this book, personal prayers, or whatever comes to mind! Just enjoy the journey and write!

_____

_____

_____

_____

_____

_____

_____

_____

_____

_____

Acknowledgements

Words can never express how grateful I am to God for allowing me to connect with author, Ruth E. Griffin. This book would not have been possible without your big push for me to just "get it done." I am also beyond indebted to Andrea L. Hines who models how to use her gift for words with eloquence. Thank you for your hugs, prayers, listening ear, and most of all words of encouragement and empowerment. You both are special ladies indeed!

About the Author

Victoria E. Henderson was born and raised in New York City, where she cultivated her love for reading and writing stories. This passion turned into messages of love and hope for her friends, who encouraged her to start her blog, "Still Waters."

Victoria knows firsthand what juggling truly means. Along with family responsibilities, Victoria serves as a Budget Analyst at a large public school district. She earned her BA in Psychology from North Carolina Central University in December of 2012 and has taken quite a few classes in pursuit of her master's in counseling.

Victoria is also a co-host on a live internet radio show with author friends, Andrea L. Hines, and Ruth E. Griffin, called Authors Up, which showcases other authors' work during interviews. The show encourages everyone in their writing with tips, timely information, and inspiration for the journey. In keeping with her encouraging spirit, Victoria posted weekly videos on Facebook and Instagram by sharing testimonies and songs that echoes her motto – "If I can help somebody, then my living shall not be in vain." She has now turned that into a live show which airs the second and fourth

Mondays of each month called "Living Life Victoriously." Both shows can be seen on ALH Broadcasting on Facebook and YouTube.

Victoria owns her own business called Victoria's Treasure Box. She sells beautiful and affordable Paparazzi jewelry to her customers who she calls Treasureville. She inspires and encourages all to be their best selves inside and out.

Victoria's first book, When I Need a Word, God Speaks! was released on July 31, 2019. The accompanying journal was released in September 2021. You can get copies on Amazon, Barnes & Noble, or wherever books are sold online. Check out her blog at www.victoriaehenderson.com where you can sign up and receive email notification when the new ones hit.

Victoria resides in North Carolina where she enjoys spending time with her family, watching her children become who they want to be, and especially, worshipping God in all circumstances.